SCISSOR, PAPER, WOMAN

SCISSOR, PAPER, WOMAN

Marianne Bluger

PENUMBRA PRESS

CANADIAN CATALOGUING IN PUBLICATION DATA

Bluger, Marianne
    Scissor, paper, woman

(Penumbra Press poetry series ; 47)
Poems.
ISBN 1-894131-01-0

    I. Title II. Series.

PS8553.L85S35 2000   C811'.54   C00-900854-3
PR9199.3.B555S35 2000

ACKNOWLEDGEMENTS

The publisher gratefully acknowledges the support of the Canada
Council for the Arts for its publishing programme.

for *LARRY*

*Way out there where words jump
in the haze
is the land of hot mamas.*

– Denise Levertov

CREDITS

Acta Victoriana; Bywords; Canadian Author; C.V.2; Event; The Fiddlehead; The Gristmill; The Malahat Review; The Nashwaak Review; Poetry Canada Review; Trail & Landscape; The New Quarterly; Vintage 95

The epigraph is from the poem "An Ignorant Person" by Denise Levertov, *With Eyes in the Back of Our Heads,* New Directions, New York, 1958.

Front cover artwork is the collage of a painting by Maji Kim and a photograph by Larry Neily.

Thanks to the Regional Municipality of Ottawa-Carleton for a grant to write poetry.

Books by Marianne Bluger

The Thumbless Man

On Nights Like This

Gathering Wild

Summer Grass

Tamarack & Clearcut

Gusts (Selected Tanka)

Scissor, Paper, Woman

CONTENTS

Present Things

Notes

FOR THE READER

THE VERY SPOT[1]

Imagine the theatre folks imagine
yourselves in the dark
hitching on prickly plush
as you watch a made-up woman
read you this

A man in the first row
the portly impresario
leaps to his feet
shakes his fist and shouts
poets are parasites

& the woman with him
bejewelled in loosened furs
with wisps of blond hair and worry
playing over her beauty
pales shrieks *Stop*
tugs the tail of his tux ...

Look look the streaming lights
are dancing with us motes

We got here by chance
just minding our business
sauntered through town
dazed a little dreamy perhaps
half-lost who knows
maybe quite lost ...

When all at once by the Bank Street bridge
we spotted the map in a plexiglass case
a set-up
by the Ministry of Culture

With an x on the spot
t read *You are here*
and we opened the door
demused distracted yes

admit this ...
But the thought appealed
(though it also appalled)
that we had been found
by nameless strangers

So here we all are in a stage drama set
in a theatre bathed in matinée light

The reader peers blind
into hot white glare
there's the rustling stir
a cough here and there

That guy in the tux
the girl in the fox
every soul in the place
with a role to play

Just watch us

NIGHT STATION

A GIRL WITH HAIR

A girl with hair streaming the fall
she turns eighteen
carts tomes of poems
in old brocaded languages
up an iron spiral stair
in the revolution that is late
sixties Montreal

For the solid heft the secret
promise in her arms
she studies them until it's spring
and her eyes are rimmed with a fine red rim

Then winter-pale trips down
as sun hits skin
to walk the gritty gleaming streets
moving her lips she chants

> I've read the Wisdom
> books where sages say
> stay sober deep
> old wall-eyed Whale keep
> dark and sane be
> melancholy and forever free
>
> Hold yourself aloof
> resolved and unbeguiled
> as that king[2] did
> who grumbled as he drank
> his daily wormwood ...
>
> (And because it's Lent[3])
> Nix once and nix again
> on all of them
> Let the green flame
> sizzle some other
> witless phoenix

But the fiercer her psalms
the hotter her body burns

And a raw squeal intolerably shrill
tears loose from the base
as her heart beats – just
the beak-tap of that frenzied bird
which squawking cracks
its brittle script-scratched
shell and bursts
dazed and dazing forth

Merciless and sharp
its claws sink deep
in youth's flushed flesh

They roil her blood
they jar her hard
blind pounding piston bone

> And the priest her seducer
> quips later
> No *aphrodisiac so strong*
> *as chastely resolve in the young*

NIGHT STATION

Some shock struck her conscious
catastrophe
hurled her body on the chilly sheet
where she lies alone exposed
to waking strangeness

Branding the darkness
red clock digits
change

while past the gauze curtain
in noumenal night the moon
lost and mysteriously dangerous
diffuses a diminished radiance
through cloudy industrial vapours

Three bare elms
thrust into the murky sky

It is those stark limbs
astir in chalky air
which mesmerize

Their nakedness is an absolute
which seems to refer
or at least to point ...

Even if they are silent
as graves in the long summer grass
they speak
of all the stiff bodies lain out below
when it is late
very late and after
now
she remembers the dream

  A night station – empty bleak and vast
  where she waits on the platform alone
  as an avalanche of engine
  longed for and feared roars in

cyclops light blinding
ground throbbing underfoot

At the din her bones go
slack in her skin
it's angel trumpets and the end
deafens as rolling iron
thunder comes abreast of her

Hot winds hit her face
and thrown east by the blast
she hurtles through darkness

to land on her back
in the snow of a forest
      wounded
a spy in some underground war
caught at the sight of a failed rendezvous
lying splayed like an X
on some terrorist map
staring up into winter elms

SCISSOR, PAPER, WOMAN[4]

He wraps her in a smooth white
sheet of truthless words
& makes of her
a present for himself

One snip of her split
scissor tongue
would cut the paper
she's packaged in

& she wants that but
feels the weight
of her body come
hard down

It bends the blades
shatters the hinge
fractures the scissors

(there's a blood thread now
on her bitten lip)

& limp she lies
still stunned and calm
a solid
round heavy
stone in his palm

FURTHER NEWS OF THE SPINSTER SETTLER

As the naked birches blurred
at last chartreuse
as the leaves stirred later on hot August nights
as they were cast
yellow torrents underfoot
she hiked slowly back

This reversal of direction
was proof she had failed
it would be her last journey
sacrificial - a warning
and she the torch a beacon would wave
flashing danger out over the hills

Hello and good-bye
I have and don't you
travel this way

Thus she located herself for us
when splayed on hot granite
she heard the scree hit far below

when blinded with fog or rain
hooded by sweat or night
shaking with cold or fright

when she leapt a fissure
and risked the freefall
smash to madness

or with skin ripped by bramble
legs wrenched by root
she was stuck in the suck
of a bug-cloud bog

when a branch cracked near
and she thought 'bear'

the calm within her tingling skin
gauged the taut isolation rope

steady as hope
it measured the force
in each blow of dumbfounding
interior silence

Her daily aloneness
she made her white page
her thoughts preserved
were fieldnotes

Late in fall she found the dead man's gift
an abandoned canoe (– in it one boot
          muddy   cracked
          for a small foot
          terrified
          and calmed her)

From then on she travelled by water
and even when freeze-up locked her craft
and she left it lodged where the beaver slept
she kept to the river
black snake route of wind-bared ice
till she came to our village

Wild-eyed with strain she was
savage and frantic to push
back to sheltering bush

She fought when found
but we soothed and nursed her
until she was human again

Then gave her the cabin
long disused of log and stone
from the ridge it's that temple loaf
(snow for flour)
just off mainstreet by the water

It's become her cloister
the cell where she works
and sleeps and sews and prays
and writes to us

"Like a God-bent acolyte
knotted on her mat
I keep to my obsessive
prayer of the heart ...[5]

Like an agoraphobic
huddled in her coat
recite beside a preacher's perch
my litanies of not"

(And the frail streaming smoke of her wavering ink
signs the sky of town days with the script of her work)

THE SHIELD

All surfaces
are hard here
ice a long time
melting then
wind-bared dirt
in ridges on bald granite

Lichens scale it sometimes
mosses cushion
a tough-rooted spruce
might writhe from a crevice

but the soil is sparse

And these flowers
small as stars?

What tundra grows

IN THE ALLEY

Dimmed now
nearly doused by urban glare
they glimmer up there
pure and far beyond us
locals blinded here by neon

Pinprick hints of firmament
that pulse a bit and resonate
their silence
once you've noticed it
dissolve the nearer
night-shift kitchen clatter

We the young long since
in pique or rage
packed up and left
but those little fold-hand mothers
attentive as ever still hover
at the parlour window

Hieratic their obsolete orbits reflect
the past as perfect
old-time
          hometown
                    lyric ...

Such lights won me once
but were forgotten – almost
I stashed the image in a blue plush box
a matchless necklace
but the smoky pearls
(when the thread broke) rolled
forever lost
in layered scapes of cosmic dust

Dismal that distancing
though at the time it felt
as sane as gravity
reversed – just common-sense
like falling off the earth

But often in the hard nights since
on a break for breath
out in the lane I ask

Which quavering
o which thin gleam
will see me through
the broken dishes and the noise

Which star Stan and whose
calm colloquy do you suppose will rise
above the guffaws of the boys

THERAPY

With a walloping hard
slap on the back
the joke hits from behind
but erupts in her gut

& something buried deep
blows up

Unstable truth
that deep-packed explosive
convulses her nexus
her solar plexus
and there blasts from her mouth
a gusty laugh

The past escapes
the sense of it all
spins the clock on the wall

Hilarious it feels
not to be
serious
not to be caught
with your face on just
to let taut skin
go slack &   laugh

ha
   ha ha
       ha ha ha
   ha ha ha ha ha ...
(the gasping for the breath
the helpless
tears)

Two peanuts were playing in the park
and one was a salted

ANOTHER FOR THE AULD BASTARD

I watch perplexed the crowds go streaming by
I start to move but everyone stands still
(perhaps both time and motion are a lie)

I can't see planets spinning though I try
A cut that bled a girl undid my will
I wait alone and crowds go streaming by

Sometimes I think the good will never die
They'll picnic on the far side of a hill
(perhaps both time and motion are a lie)

While life is scored with just a cricket's cry
and endless waves going nowhere make me ill
I watch perplexed the crowds go streaming by

Millennia are Yahweh's single sigh
There isn't any time at all to kill
(perhaps both time and motion are a lie)

My heart fixed on your face   It blazed my eye
I thought if you were Jack I might be Jill
I watch perplexed the crowds go streaming by
(perhaps both time and motion are a lie)

THE ZEN MASTER'S WIFE

I

After years hushing infants so he
could sit in silent meditation
years sweeping rage-smashed rice bowls
migrainous years
cowering among splintered heirlooms
gathering courage to leave

After years of dire threats
nightmare years flailing
stick arms at darkness
years of courtroom terror years
of shot nerves lost in Gauloise
smoke when rough coughs
masked gasps and sobs ...

Years of confused debriefing questions
such as Why did he marry? For Lust
for Cash for Immigration?
But Why did you have him?

After years turned chaste nun imploring
the Haesychast prayer
and just holding on
to that icon in turn
with idiot routine work

After years when Only Friend
the strike-out pitcher champion
pacifist fox-kit orphan son
of the-almost-governor-of-Texas
gave up his knightly longing and was gone

After years on welfare kibitzing with ghosts
of Daddy's Nazi persecuted past
and Mother's genteel bibliographies

Background years static
and newsless except

for reports in exotic journals
which always read: "*The Master Prospers*"

After years recounting
to a man in a room in a chair
what seemed at first like a novel tale
but shot with shame
for what impulse had done to the children

One overcast morning it came
to a head on collision with the fact
that someone had been
literally shoved
in a corner and pissed on

II

suddenly one summer night
satori arrived with a radio

from my bed I could hear
jazz playing in the street
– jarring strains
a discord of strings sawing darkness

That music was

and it stopped

then someone woke
who had not been
asleep

and eyes on their optic stems
rotated ...

in the void there were stars
fire points burning
blue in the blackness

stigmata of cosmos
and a slight wind rose
stirring sultry air

Like breath it sighed
through the bamboo blind
as I watched the bars
in moonlight gently bend

NUDE WITH SCAR

WHAT HAPPENED TO THE BODY THEN

An early sunset shot gilt meaning through
that rusty centretown apartment afternoon

The violinist ended his baroque piece
which hung in the air like intrigue
then bowed in four directions:
to the sink the lamp the window
and to her ...

Mumbling disjointed compliments I left
by a wheedling wall groped the dim hall
rummaged for boots in the dark vestibule
and kicked through loose drifts to the car

There in its chill lap I sat
when the steel key had clicked
hearing the silence after

Coaxed in the end to cough
with a clunk like heaving rocks
convulsing the engine started

But only when shuddering minutes had passed
did heat clear the glass
fogged blank with my breath

And all the way home
cold engine metal rasped
while the muffler banged asphalt and ice
– like the tincans of newlyweds
it rattled attracting stares

That's all I remember of that
grim retreat except
by the Bank Street bridge
I saw a man in a turban kick
the fenderless wreck
that had stranded him there in a snowbank

IN MARCH

On her sleek neck the rain-
beads gleam
blue violet and green
as she the pink-foot pigeon rests
below a dripping bench-slat

Nor does she stir
when grinding up the slope
a city bus looms into view

It stops now
and though blank doors nictitate
one blink of reptile fate
as they slide   open
                                    shut
no one gets in or out

There's a rush of sewers filling
at the bottom of the hill
while the trees on Byron Boulevard
not yet in leaf
standing stiffly naked
wear the careful random look
of standards planted by municipal decree

NUDE WITH SCAR

In the night thunder
blood river
two seeds swim

One – soot black
jets inky death
the other – bright
spawns wriggling gamete life

But only when a scrubbed Scots surgeon
swathed to the eyes
and trained in ruthless hope
lifted his blade and cut
her blue-veined marble
milk-flesh breast
did she at last learn this
atomic secret

Into her cracked crystal eyes
gaze now and read
how late in a late
millennial nuclear age
alone and afraid
in a stainless steel hospital bed

she glimpsed that truth
which always was
the dire joy of the Greeks

BY BLUFFS

The fog's gauze
pale contagion
swathes this town
in yellow-grey oblivion

Horizon's gone

Streaming cold
drizzle the rain
snake finds her spine

as a black umbrella
one panel flashing dimly
above a man's body
approaches

And she turns
towards the park
disconsolate and sodden
almost dark

to walk the muddy track
under poplars dripping
by a granite cliff

And there there advances
loping towards her head down
the first live thing today
(besides that faceless man)
she's come upon

a drenched mongrel
dog cocks his head
to favour his single eye
one oblique second
peers her way

then drops his soaked muzzle
growls deep in his shivering
belly and twists
back off into bush

TERRIFIED ODE

I entered a doll's house
built to human scale
a Victorian marvel complete in detail
to the frigate knocker
and lacquered portrait
above the mantel on a silver nail

The furniture gleaming on heirloom Tabriz
was curly mahogany – impossible to move
and the woman there on the fringed divan
a spinster the very age I am

Behind her there figured a wall of pale orchids
cut I surmised with cuticle scissors
from paper and pasted on ebony silk

All marched the diagonal
but one positioned by a sconce
not découpage was real
a little yellowed and collapsing like a lung

The test I'd been set was to notice
neatly displayed but cunningly hid
in that period room
the decay of one
sedately rotting bloom

I gasped
so I passed

The woman poured tea
which arched streaming
into shell-thin cups
(Limoges I think – with shamrocks)
then buttered a scone
and blushing revealed
the investments she held on the Dow

And when our ritual communion was through
in fraught regal tones
she spoke what I most had been dreading to learn –
that I would be asked to return

PORCHLIGHT

Glare-cast black on brick
the birch in the wind last night
when I got back alone to the house
shuffled shadow cards
in the deck of death

And a powdery moth
as I had once
fluttered helpless there
by the door where that signal
bulb you had left
in the troubling dark
of no comfort or use
was burning cold and false

But I being changed
and no longer sister
to that poor doomed
blindly bumping creature

by feel alone took from my purse
the cold steel key
an agent stranger once had given me
and let myself into the place

THE LETTER
– for a teen suicide

A cicada drills the stone
quiet of an empty street

now and then there's a car

but the creak of porch wicker
measures this hour

heavy with fate
as she rocks it is
stretching forever

so that she remembers exactly
how it felt to be a child –

      alive   breathing   open
      waiting   a little afraid

      What will they decide?

But no longer a child as she reads
in the hard glare she knows
at last and for sure
that there are intrigues complex
as novel-plots maps with directions
to fixed destinations plans
of the place where they think she should be
agreed on beforehand approved
in her absence
                resistance
is futile the battle with parents
turned to a ritual
combat with strangers unnatural
conflict for which she was not meant

she has no weapon – love
is not a weapon
and she has no argument

The rage that hurled objects
smashed on the wall
of their calmly intelligent
white-lipped will
stilled in the end

she had done as they wished

And so it seems clear
that the future is theirs
she will simply oblige
with the fury of meekness
dumb logic demands

return to the cellar

return to that womb
to the cord
to the chair with
one kick at the air

be born again elsewhere
or nowhere

and why should she fear
now she's chosen to leave them
the silence they always
demanded of her

THE SKY A SALMON RIVER

Some asters
smoky mauve in cold bright air
breath visible now
drifting   frost ...
and past the weather-beaten shed
a maple wielding boughs of fire

Space you wanted – distance
the Big Lonely The
real emptiness
and chose for your November break
such thick-set bush of north Québec
as verges closing on the rapid water
and glinting boulders of the Godbout River

For paradise – your paradox
the peace of the as yet
unsettled
lets you cast
squinting into the glitter
for that shimmering dream
fish you angle for
that rosy salmon

With a clatter of fibreglass tentrods
cameras and coolers you made to leave
prepared as though sure
yours was the only odyssey

Fetching forgotten candles and salt
I smiled bereft like Penelope left

But worst was your last return to the house
for that tin of winter hand-tied flies
you emerged with it clutched
to your checked flannel chest
and laid it with care where I
had we managed a truce might have sat
beside you on the right front seat

then gave me a peck climbed into the truck
and drove away waving good-bye with the map

The kid's off to camp I thought
hit by a slight
resentment at abandonment

But don't imagine when you see this poem
printed in some magazine
that I scorn your solitary enterprise
La Pêche

I who each day when you're home
every day when you're gone still lift
the red canoe myself
on thin ropy shoulders and manage
another tricky portage

or alone encamped remain
for hours in purling shoals
fishing for metaphors ...

know it for mine as well
this wilful journey
sole adventure and only trek
down a blind trail to interior black

Like you I often stop
panting exhausted terrified lost
combing marsh-reed scanning bush
for any gap that might lead past
the darkening that has me blocked

And this morning as well
alone in the chill
with my bones and my breath
under rolling cloud
chase hard blown thoughts

On the very spot
where you launched yourself
as Merwin did and Atwood

and Purdy and the rest
who also risked
a lonely death by drowning

THE RED RIM

BEACH WITH JENNY MISSING

The tide's been out and in
and out again like dresser drawers
a thousand times
but she's still gone

– the one who used to lope along this beach
by shell shards and wet seaweed strands
such reckless purpose in her face
such sweetness in her wailing voice
we never thought to challenge
her determined indirection
or examine the scar signatures
her naked feet left on the pinkish sand

> *The seasons run*
> *along their hectic track*
> *from rain to heat*
> *from mist to wind and back*

In hopes that she might come
Harlan at the Clam & Mussel Diner
now in slow mid-afternoon
is at the window watching:

a few blurred strangers pass
and more and more
the fog rolls in
against the glass

She used to flash a fragile smile at him
but he like we who thought we knew her then
can't think what he should do
or might have done ...

She has become a sort of goddess in the telling
and locals still recount their sightings
of her floating hair her reaching
swinging swaying arms regretting

that they didn't set their work aside that day
and follow when she passed beyond the quay

THE SAVOURERS

Past the shimmering
asphalt snake
that glides without moving
along the coast

past the big blind
billboards ranged
by gas-bars and fried clam joints

& further yet
past sagging fences
like spent elastic
trussing cottage yards

on out beyond the wind-swept marsh
with its swaying fringe
of seagrass – down

the embankment
along bare dunes
over the misting silver flats

past one last wave
of ocean wrack
that curve of tidal detritus

at dusk

when the air grows clear
liquid and purer than water

they pass
with their aunts and their dogs
the genteel savourers
over the cold firm sand

THE RED RIM[8]

The high sun beats
its brazen gong
so the others leave
but you

just wave and turn
and stride right in
letting cold ocean
climb your pale thighs
shuddering when it laps your waist

And now you brace yourself to lunge
but the bottom shifts
horizon tips heaving water
knocks you off your legs

and you founder
in the tremendous
salubrious dark sea

Flotsam on glitter
a white and bulbous lump
of dumpling flesh
that sharp waves slap

you gasp as lacy sea-foam slips
along your limbs
then slides across the oily
muscled torso of the deeps

Caught now bound
in hard embrace
you struggle
as massed water pulls
you under and the wheeling
sky above is
closing almost
everything is over ...

Here on panic's hook you thrash
while some black box recording this

catastrophe won't stop –
your own shelled ear
gathering signals
keeps hearing
the rush of eternal news

rising and falling surf
pounds meaning
the breakers roar

And what they are roaring is Yes
Let female be fish

Brine stings your lips
it blears your eyes
and you writhe at every
onslaught of a wave

The gulls overhead
wheedle *surrender*

Defeated in answer
you open
your throat
wide as a salmon
and breathe
water in

Sweat rains then hard on your skin
and tears – remember those
unforecast downpours
awkward   random   warm

welling they pour
with that savour of salt
you have tasted before

And here daughter
in the flash of a fin
that grim disparity between
the voracious ultramarine
and your gillless body seems

not quite so tragic

now that you know
there is nothing to know
the terror slackens easily
you let go

Jetsam still on an alien sea
but piscine woman too
whose drama unfolds
in the watery hold
of primal gravity

And though you may not ever see again
your cottage natal shore or kin
each cell thrills
to the coded recall
of the soft-bellied finny
creature you once were
before ever you slithered
up onto mud from the deeps

And lightened by a cosmic wind
the gentle breath of *caritas*[9]
you float
face bared to the sky
simply drift

Clouds roll past
but harmless now
those beasts of myth

With undulant ocean
your medium won
you are riding your own
late-come evolution

Bubbles break
like laughter on the surface
reed fronds slimed pod strands
which neither strangle nor enchain
adorn your limbs in mermaid dress

Shimmering water sheens
down your flanks and light-
fanned spectrums are your shining scales

Rolling like a porpoise
onto your chest
you carve your path
through swinging troughs

A re-creation this
immersion in benignant blue-green
restorative innocent healing
a baptism
the ancient struggle easily reversed
some kind of holy returning

And though you wrestle now
you do succumb to being
tipped bobbed tossed
risking all in the swell
as a woman risks well
letting go even when
she cleaves to her man

And so by hope by tide propelled
by the honest homing
dove of will
you swim with the strength of ten
until one flailing-not
-flailing hand
grazes land:
          the sandbar shallows
of a cove so calm
it seems unlikely there was ever danger

And lifting yourself
leaden with streaming
water chains tugging every limb
you dragstep in

grunting exhausted
cross kelp-hung rocks

the spray-dimmed flats
all sketched with tidal detritus
                            to rest

Easing down on hot sand
shivering a little in the noonday sun
you lean on your elbow
and gaze at the level horizon

You bask there a while
composed and at peace
rejoice   in your vision
(fixed on that village
winking down the coast)

rejoice at this last
near-drowning the just
once more revealed
blessèdness of disaster

(as your sight grows
steadily sharper now
clearing
as after long weeping)

LOUISE IN THE KITCHEN
(CRAB COVE)

In her Maritime way
which is slow   savouring
she gauges the scene

slouched by the fridge
in a shaft of sun
half lost in thought half
listening
        to cries ring in
through the cabin screen
– gulls and squealing
at their robber games
the children
            making the most
            of their holiday freedom

She turns to a cupboard below the stairs
takes her paintbox and easel
unwraps a fresh canvas
        (as from yellowing tissue
        in the attic once
        she lifted a christening dress
        – her maiden aunt's –

        white as this page on her lap it lay
        soft in the slant light there
        and warm as though slipped minutes since
        from infant shoulders

        every detail of that silk feather-stitchery
        shone in the stillness
        sharp and real
        as a fossil fern
        just prised from a book of shale

        Why when first she lifts a brush
        does she always recall
        that virginal brightness?)

She unscrews three tubes
daubs what she needs
and begins with the given:
remains of lunch

six green glass plates
a bread-heel the pickle jar (half-full
of curling gold-green cuke and onion)
a bowl of luminous melon scraps
the Woolworth jug with four smudged glasses
the perennial ketchup John's pewter mug
her old rose cup and the clutter of silver

all as her family left them scattered
round a ragged beach-pea and lupin bouquet
on the slightly askew
faded Delft blue cloth

Subject enough again today
are present things
'At the Cottage, Crab Cove'

She will paint what is
in the light she has
paint the light
and the light is love

GODZERO THE GORILLA (METRO ZOO)[10]

Blue-black is the colour
of his fur – no not fur – hair
as slightly pigeon-toed he lurches
forward in his cage
dragging log legs
as though world weights
were fastened on each foot

Red-eyed as a rubby it's true
he's right here more or less intact
from some green steamy tract
of jungle in possibly Kenya

where his foremothers swung
along lush paths in joy and mated
with their kind then licked
and preened and nursed
their staring young

and there reposed   being natural
as noble savage
          normal primates are ...

He scratches his nipple his flank
picks at his navel and slowly
spreads his thick Mick Jagger lips
in something like a grimace
          – not a grin

then lets his hapless helpless arms hangs down
disconsolate as though hacked off
with flattened curved
sharp hookings at the end
adangle in some vaguely troubling wind

His head hangs too
perpetually low
but lifted and poked forward on its ropy stem
the nape of that tough corded neck's a thing
most poignant   It speaks of age

and uselessness and pride
and how the vulnerable stand
easiest to hit below the skull
high up and from behind

His coat is thinning and some hairs are white
there's shiny rump skin showing through
wrinkled and pinkish bared from sitting
listless years on concrete
by a green trapdoor
(making her think of Eldred
who's a civil service clerk)

Godzero (as she's named him) peers
a while out through the bars
then turns away
quite unashamed to be
bored with the beetle-browed woman
who gapes at him in such alarm

Why trembles she why seems
so shocked to learn how quickly
yet how tenderly has grown
her fondness for this dislocated ape

Why feels she blessed
by his indifference
unless she be an Eden innocent
whom he has just dismissed
as harmless ...

And her unsteady heart grows warm
at his benignant captive unconcern

IZUMI SHIKIBU[11]

Pale   naked   Sappho
moon   woman of Japan
breasting the night clouds
you swim steep heaven alone

and when with those thin sharp cusps
your porcelain arms you rake
the heaving back of that dark refusal
who is your ocean lover

all the dunes from envy
slip into the water

PRESENT THINGS

PRESENT THINGS[6]

There is the corpse of something
like an effigy of her
stuffed with wood-fibre
propped by rods standing
on perpetual exhibit at the Nature Museum

And as though some loss might be prevented
the bird has been mounted
wired to alarms in a theft-proof glass cabinet

A passenger for once that pigeon
dazed and weak from shifting winds
folded her wings and hid
in the steam-warmed chink of a black locomotive

The engine stamped "1914"[7]
was the one that carved woodlands
the one that sliced prairies and ran
roping mountains and ribboning canyons with iron

The one that shrieked punctual warning
down all the sundrunk summer days
and howled baleful threats
through dark and long and lonely winter nights

The one that went leaving the immigrant
all his worldly goods cast
around him in satchels
on remote station platforms
the one that trailed echoes in empty valleys
and a signature of smoke ...

The one that would skirt
the salt-sprayed coast at last
and turn and begin
unravelling the country again

It carried her into the country
we're headed for
the future
now
we know she flew before us

That hot-blood bird lived by fast desire
for seeds for berries
then fuelled on them ravaged
crop-fields and orchards

Consuming all fruiting earth she raced
in hungry migratory twisters
nevermind winters summer droughts bad harvests

Heedless she was
madness feathered
an impetuous blitz of appetite
farmers hated her species near numerous
as all other birds combined

And so in a rage
for sport or feathers
for the taste of her meat
the world took aim
and shot

Sleek-necked and amber-eyed
with a russet breast and mottled mantle
in fragile abundance
she flourished once
on earth with us

But only lately have we come to mourn
the savage passage
of that common dove
whose glory was
the love of present things

THE SHOESTORE

When I tell sensible Joan how stymied I am
she says *Go where you want*
Love isn't anything – isn't
for instance bigger than a breadbox
and *men aren't worth the grief*

God knows the woman's bright
survived a hard past trusting only her wits
and gets on with life while I drift around lost ...

There's the place – that corner shop
where Eros' wing the day you loomed
through falling flakes and overcoats
first touched my heart

I remember we stood blinking snow from our lashes
discussing brave Quincey who'd died
and Gerald who's decent and lies for his wife

a channel of tenderness
wide as the Fundy opened between us
as astonished   dismayed
we fell into silence

It was a silence vast as all outdoors
through which the ganging buses lurched
belching exhaust and pelting slush
on two there plunged in awkwardness ...

until in the end mumbling shaken *goodbyes*
we set off – each for the rest of life

It's been a bad month since
and the danger has probably passed
but Ottawa's so changed
that just to get my bearings
I look for the shoestore

And everything's strange now
even the streetnames
though this is the town I grew up in

AT THE DRYCLEANERS

It must have been that fast drug hope
hit near the arborite counter
there by the cash when we met
two weeks gone Wednesday at Cleanrite
because the trouble
flared right away again

Instantly flushed
I grappled with hanger hooks
and plastic film
then dropped my purse

you picked it up but then
such dizzying confusion reigned
that mumbling a strangled good-bye
I rushed for home without the fruit
and having forgotten to go to the bank

I remember I climbed the back-stairs in a daze
and still in my coat
fell limp across the unmade bed

let the gloom gulp me down
let it swallow me whole
an oyster one life in the sea
of distant household sounds

Only scattering shells
glimmered past curtains and doors
as my limp abandoned arms
dissolved in laving
waves of nothing I was
drifting deeps of empty peace ...

Yes as I say it's fourteen days since
and though we shared hardly a word
in the cold fluorescent glare of that store
a glance of mine spoke
and you seemed to hear ...

while you in turn revealed
abashed but whole
with an anguished smile
freed of its soiled clothes
your naked soul

BLESSÉ[12]

Shadows are long and the weary
slope of your back
seems to fit
some harness of duty

gravity
inclines your body down
keeps pulling you home
as leaning on your shovel you go on
like a highway
in that tired monotone
claiming you never aimed
for happiness ...

You've been bent from youth on misery
it's the thing next to the soil
you've longest trusted

and nothing I can think to say
gives comfort

So here in the garden
late in the day we stand
at the same old impasse once again:
silence
which you hear as *grief wins*

       in the void
       with evening falling
       emptiness begins

Well emptiness is nothing
but that nothing
challenges

and in sad defeated peace
we hear each other breathing

Now a breeze starts up
slurred speech

a little bravura flurry in the leaves

while over your shoulder
the sun goes
sliding low behind a cone-hung spruce
laying its gold upon the outstretched limbs

And above us all around
the handsome pines
black now shaped against the blaze
are silhouettes that seem
to have made the slow breast-strokes
of swimmers in time

– seem for a moment sublime
and though darkling
noble as your stalwart heart
against the flaming glory

AVISON[13]

Earth scent - that spirit
smoke of life still clings
to the leaves she gathers:
leathery oak luminous beech
       rough elm   limp glowing maple ...

Above her in flame
canopies floats time
suspended in October air
a silence that crowns her
like Pentecost fire[14]

this blaze is hers
a timeless pyre
to savour now
or kindle later

when she will stoke her cabin grate
with fuel she's cut for the burning work

Then tinder will catch
the bark ignite
the pith wood flare

and then the conflagration roar
and her wan face flush
her sharp eyes blear
with smoke or pity
they will tear

as she takes each leaf
by the stem – like this
and burns her scraps
of gathered glory
one by one to ash

She will tap the soft powder after
from a trough of paper
into a burnished altar urn

and we who come at our leisure later
to lift the trumpet-angel lid
on her gold censer's captured truth

will find again the autumn woods
and sealed intact an incense
from the district of our youth

CELADON

In the cool still
pale rain-rinsed
pre-dawn

I woke to find you owned
the breath rising
falling in me ...

and redbird heart
he of flooding wingstroke
in his trinket cage of bone
yours alone

dazed I rose
slipped a silk dress on
pinned my hair high
and caught the bus downtown

I found you there
in the hub of that maze
where your office is
and watched you poised
with your head in your hands
lost among points on a map of Qatar

Though a figment of my longing
fell across your back
you did not stir

Now as I laze with swimming eyes
limp in your arms
I recall Chuang's[15] dream
of a butterfly

skimming clover in the blazing day
high in air in light set free
lifted drifting into summer heaven

maybe only dreaming
we ...

GULF

A rumble shook me in the vacant night
not thunder building in the Gatineau
not land being blasted
nor the roar of surf on rock

no tremor in some Shield-fault underground
and not late transport traffic leaving town ...

more like percussion
that racket when it broke
was sweetly crazy
as the start-up sound of jazz

lowdown with discordant throbs
gently jolting gutsy

music – and it shot
gladness ringing through my lonesome bones
aching from distance stiff with lack
when you called to say
you'd catch the next plane back

SKIN

By my desk
just brushing the fine
mesh window screen
when a breeze stirs in
there's an almond bush
where finches have nested
so close
that the strands of their song
have woven this late-spring poem

IN *ALBION DAYLIGHT*[16]

Everything went
white over-
exposed
in the nuclear flash

& these are the words of one collapsed
who afterwards   grown cancerous
confined to bed
wrote in a stainless steel hospital
cabinet copy of Albion Daylight:
   In this journal '&' is the hub
   and the man loves the woman
   because the woman loves the man
   because love is eternal
   there is no cause

   everything simply proceeds

   & in that light
   the pure light of radical thought
   which settles on the hawthorn
   each twig ignites and the whole tree lifts
   its thousand orange-hearted
   white candle blooms to the wind

   from faroff it's Yahweh's fiery cloud
   signal for reverence obedience   fear
   and at last your feet track holy ground

   you know your feet track holy ground

   & in that journal it is always now
   but always soon to be winter
   deep frozen blackness
   when even the steamy-breathed animals sleep

   & the dark breeding terror
   awakens what must ever after
   be illumined by the present
   fires of the unforgotten

& in that book the warning stands written
that I would not nor you
survive the failure of love

there is an entry under 'surrender'
how it must be total   remember
the battle we waged to establish
whose was the more steadfast
refusal of happiness

& then how we had to forgive

on this page floats our cabin home

anchorless in air adrift
on hazed blue – smoke or mist
which daylight at daybreak shall cleave

& the motes there circulating catch
the sun shafts of molecular imagination
which flashing gift for magnification
never can know boredom

roll the pages with your thumb
feel the wind soft on your skin
heart's doe
swishing through bracken

& it's sunset   now
blazing that glory
train passing through town
all its flatcars freighted
down with gold   each bearing one
eternity at a time

& that wind gently raising
each hair on your arm
blowing where it listeth (I told you
it was breath) –
speaks the holy language

you hear it and laugh
& once you have read what you find
in that journal you change

see how I have become
the one who survived her own death
and it was nothing

DEATH SEATED

Wheezing *Leave your wash on the line to wave*
harmless flags for the tiny republic
underground nations of the domestic
he beckons her to a folding chair
under lilac fading behind the house

And *Pity* blames *You never come*
when the petal-fall of the crab was snow
when lilies bent in wilting folds
when poppies bled in breathless heat
and phlox gave up its heady scent ...

till those staunch mums you praise in print
at last succumbed
and snow itself banked every bed
I watched alone

She had always known he haunted her yard
with his vegetal smile of faint reproval
and often before had glimpsed his back

but today in the rustling shade she sits
for the first time after illness calm
close enough to hear him speak
to feel the gust of his windy laugh

for the first time close enough to sense
innocent leaf-smoke on his breath

AFTER STEIN[17]

Pebble-skinned the navel-ended
one for tarts plus tea wedge two
now sunshine hits rock three
dories on the dazzle   sea?

But when comes winter
blank Ontario sorrow
and heedless art class
louts bump crowing
glowing snowblind through
all keen to paint
chrome yellow with shadow their shade
hits and this brash fruit sits
disconsolate if it could think
what's good what's true
smeared sadly green with blue ...

And then from downtown
maestro brats storm in
wanting fast themes and score
juggling their throats they coax
astringent notes
                    but the racket knocks
my elliptical lovely
mutes with a bruising
                    tump off the shelf
And have you not read those dusty-shouldered
sincerely sincere philosophers
who first squeeze an essence
of citric acid out
then print the equivalent
nullity left: six sad skins
and clouds in a glass
I am sorry to say it 'invalid piss'

o don't

and haven't any of you guessed
the mercy of quiet
and a lover who lets me express
my already thank-you quite lemons

IN APRIL

Convalescent stooped and slow
advancing through her muddy yard
she finds sharp shoots
have pierced the melt-drenched loam
          & down the road
          awakened
          meadows tremble in the wind

Narcotic greens
narcotic greens
like reeling firmaments disclose
in their appearing randomness
the sweetest means that you or she
or any wandering Thales[18] might
choose to be
wonder-struck with
at the moment
when we die

Remember him in old Miletus?
agape below unscrolling stars
he cartwheeled off a cliff
to his last surprising
death in moon-white seas

& crippled Patchen?
like some Zorba dancing on an empty beach
in his mad calm astonished
at catastrophe
whirled round hard and held
his very death in close embrace

until he shouted in his croaking voice
at sunset one cloud-riven day
'Hallelujah anyway'
the finest phrase that I have ever read

Keats coughed
blood verse

& Takuboku too
scribbled tanka
one for each last
rattling breath

so by a small-town patch of ground
spiked with sharp unfurling tips
in April now she sends you this
grass-stained letter no return address ...

> *on mainstreet – lamplit*
> *the crown of an ailing elm*
> *stirs all night long*

NOTES

1. There is a passage by V. S. Naipaul in *The Mystic Masseur* (Andre Deutch, London, 1957) which reads: "Is like watching a theatre show and then finding out afterwards that they was really killing people on the stage." p. 126.

2. Mithridates of classical antiquity was reputed to have taken daily small doses of poison to inure his body to attempts on his life.

3. Lent is the penitential season of fasting and prayer before Easter.

4. In the game of 'scissor, paper, rock,' two face each other. At the count of three, each raises one hand: scissor (two fingers) cuts paper; paper (hand open) wraps rock; rock (a fist) breaks scissors.

5. The prayer of the Haesychasts (Russian Orthodox quietists) is "Lord Jesus Christ, have mercy on me."

6. Based on a reading of "On a Monument to the Pigeon," a passionate elegiac essay on the passenger pigeon, by Aldo Leopold in *A Sand County Almanac*, Oxford University Press, 1949.

7. Presumed year of extinction of *Ectopistes migratorium* – the Passenger pigeon.

8. A poem for my daughter.

9. Sweet charity.

10. After Elizabeth Bishop's poem, "The Man-Moth."

11. Japanese tanka poet (A.D. 974-1034).

12. Meaning *wounded* (in French) but bearing the sense of blessed to an English ear.

13. Margaret Avison.

14. Pentecost fire was the flame of the Holy Spirit which descended on the disciples to comfort and empower them after the death and resurrection of Christ.

15. On waking from dreaming he was a butterfly, Chuang was not sure whether he was Chuang awakened or the butterfly dreaming he was Chuang.

16. Kenny Patchen wrote his mad novel, *The Journal of Albion Daylight*. This title is in tribute to him and to his visionary take on catastrophes of all description.

17. Gertrude Stein.

18. Thales was curious and dreamy and met his death by walking over a cliff while marvelling at the stars, a demise I have always respected.

PENUMBRA PRESS

PENUMBRA PRESS POETRY SERIES # 47

Poems typeset in 10.5 pt. Sabon, folios in Stempel Garamond

Old Style. The text stock is Clarion 400 Cream.

Printed in Canada for Penumbra Press in an edition of 500 copies

by AGMV Marquis.